Advance Praise for

WHAT COMES *of* WAITING

In KB Ballentine's new book, *What Comes of Waiting*, poems form a radiant narrative rich with sensory images, noun and verb surprises and the flash of sudden statement, all deeply grounded in the natural world's power. The poems create a cycle, a journey of four sections. The first renders daughter poems flavored with love, change, worry and faith; like geese, a young adult away from home knows the direction of her flight. In the second section a winter storm emerges in which natural settings mirror an inscape of abandonment, loneliness, and loss, yet not without survival and the courage to change. In the finale sections a resurrection follows, burdens fall away, and a woman honed sharp by her own personal crucible arises to find new love. Like life, Ballentine's collection creates a dark enchantment, but not without color, light and her skillful belief in the transformative power of language.

— Bill Brown, Author of *Late Winter* and *The News Inside*

In *What Comes of Waiting*, KB Ballentine weaves alchemical word magic with an astounding tenderness in vision and voice. Her poems are elegant jewels, with a powerful sense of place in the Appalachian mountains. Her vision is sometimes devastating, and always full of a sensual beauty, transparent emotions, and language that sings. KB is a master of unusual and expressive verbs, giving texture to inner and outer worlds, with subtext even more powerful than the words. Her poems will call you to see the world in a different way."

— Diane Frank, Author of *Blackberries in the Dream House*

In *What Comes of Waiting*, KB Ballentine creates a living organism of voices—both *dark* ("a phrase, a river/molecules of grief compounded into an alphabet that presses like lead"), and *light* (natural, as well as human incandescence)—that "scald[s] away scented shadows." Ballentine's third collection is a symphony of sound and meaning in which, I am sure, its readers will find much beauty and elucidation for many years to come among "shadows nudging stone//a rake forgotten against the shed, fingers/etched like rails upon the wood// . . . [a] car creeping in driveway, twin beams blind//clouds stretching, bruising the sky//a lighted rectangle opening, closing." *What Comes of Waiting* is a poetry of quest and substance. *What Comes of Waiting* is its own reward.

— Terry Lucas, author of *If They Have Ears to Hear*

WHAT COMES
of WAITING

Books by KB Ballentine

Fragments of Light (2009), Celtic Cat Publishing
Gathering Stones (2008), Celtic Cat Publishing

Anthologies containing her work:

Southern Poetry Anthology, Volume VI: Tennessee (2013)
Southern Light: Twelve Contemporary Southern Poets (2011)
A Tapestry of Voices (2011)

WHAT COMES
of WAITING

KB BALLENTINE

BLUE LIGHT PRESS ❧ 1ST WORLD PUBLISHING

1ST WORLD
PUBLISHING

SAN FRANCISCO | FAIRFIELD | DELHI

1st World Publishing
PO Box 2211
Fairfield, Iowa 52556
www.1stworldpublishing.com

Blue Light Press
1563 45th Avenue
San Francisco, California 94122

Cover and Page Design, Author Photo
Jim Canestrari

Cover Photo
Vanessa McLaughlin

☞

ISBN: 978-1-4218-8671-8

Library of Congress Control Number: 2013912023

Publication Acknowledgements

The author would like to thank the following publications in which some of these poems were previously published:

String Poet, Alehouse, River of Earth and Sky: Poems for the 21st Century, New Millennium Writings, Tidal Basin Review, Prime Mincer, Sugar Mule, New Mirage, Mary: A Journal of New Writing, The Tennessee Writer, String Poet, Front Range, Writer's Digest, Still, Cuivre River Anthology, and *American Diversity Report.*

FOR JIM...

and those who take second chances

FORWARD

Some people flow in and out of our lives like water — rushing through like a stream, surrounding us like a peaceful lake then maybe traveling on to the sea. Some people are more like rocks: sturdy, stable, reliable — always there. Everyone we meet informs our sensibilities of the larger world around us, not allowing us to become so absorbed that we forget ourselves in this mad-dash through life.

This collection of poems introduces the reader to people who voluntarily leave us as well as those we lose without their choice, much sooner than we would wish. The later poems embrace the people who endure, those who stay with us through sorrow and joy. I would like to thank all these people, for, without them, this collection would not have been possible.

I am grateful to the following individuals and groups for encouraging and supporting me in my writing life: my husband, Jim; my parents, Buddy and Susan; Diane Frank and the Blue Light Press writing workshop participants; Bill Brown; Terry Lucas; Helga Kidder; Karen Slikker; Jeff Ferrell; Kristi Walker; David Austin; Connie Landreth; my creative writing students; my Open Mic group; Chattanooga Writers Guild; Knoxville Writers Guild; Colrain Poetry Manuscript Conference participants; the Lesley University community.

Thank you for being my strong rocks or flowing water. You are the sources of my inspiration.

Contents

I.

II.

III.

IV.

I.

STORING UP

Huckleberries rumple mountain base,
black at twilight, purple at noon.
Autumn infuses
the oak, the maple — greens sparking into fires
of gold, red. Desire. Indian summer beguiles

us with warmth. We shut our eyes, ignore
the transformation. Sunlight prances through thinning
leaves, exposes twisted trunks, calloused knots.
A curious turn of frost hardens the earth —

crows stab through white, argue with the wind.

WORMWOOD

Because the wind was in the East
we forgot to breathe, forgot to watch
the sun's tendrils stroke bronze and gold
from fading blue.
                     And when night tripped
into place, moon's song calling light
out of darkness, we cursed the hearts
that still beat, the hope that dared squirm

 even as we devoured the marrow from their bones.

To the Neighbors, Who Leave Their Cats to Starve Each Summer

The dog spots her first — black scrap
of fur, rheumy-eyed and skittish.
She cringes then scuttles, her scabby
kitten tagging down the sloping yard.

Zeeta snuffs the grass, whines more excited.
Gnats spiral evening air, swollen sun
shrinking with the heat. In the beetled garden
sunflowers shelter a mangled sparrow.

Flies drone and purr over unblinking eye,
wings severed from body, brown belly
gnawed open. Red escapes onto blistered
grass. Neck drawn back, beak opens

in soundless evensong. Geraniums and impatiens
droop, fade into graying twilight. Green eyes
flicker behind a deck chair. Across the yard,
the Kerr's vacant carport yawns wide,

porch light scalding the gathering shadows.

GÖTTERDAMMERUNG

twilight of the gods

And in these last days the sun still warms
the earth, downy woodpecker tapping
the oak under slanting light. Webs,
white and silky, reach from tree to tree.
Skunks stripe the forest floor, shadow ferns.

Starlings stare from birch, butternut,
yellow eyes watching. Guarding.
Two squirrels dash into the yard,
leaping and tunneling grass
grown tall against molding walls.
A tricycle rusts the cracked carport.

Rope broken, ragged, a tire swing rots
its ring as autumn leaves scratch
the wind. Splintered and faded, empty
feeders dangle from a drooping porch.
Doves huddle, waiting.

TELOS

the end

Over Lake Michigan, the plane
winks in noon light. A heron stretches wings —
shock of white in the blue sky,
blue water stitching this day.

Beneath oak and poplar, acorns dot
a flaming mantle withering to brown.
Sacrifices of the season. Evergreens lean
with the wind, limbs trembling.

Sun slips, clouds brisk the sky. A fisherman
casts a ripple that echoes to shore.
The pole slopes, shadow bobbing waves —

memories that growl from a primal past.
A branch of fate as it arcs the wind,
settles into the hand of man.

I Never Heard My Grandmother Sing

An alphabet's molecules,/ tasting of honey, iron and salt. — Jane Hirschfield

A letter, a leaf
      her thoughts spiral to childhood's
      barefoot trudge to school
      pausing at the creek to wash sleep's salt
      before the '30s dusted the land, left grit in the teeth.

A word, a stone
      war bride hides fear, hangs cloth
      on lines ranged like battlefronts
      throat rusted shut to the honey,
      the vinegar of her baby's birth, death.

A phrase, a river
      molecules of grief compounded
      into an alphabet that presses like lead
      on her chest, her heart —
      an ocean choking the notes of her song.

A Farther Shore

A gull dozes under the noon sun,
tucked against his rocky roost. Wind whistles
through fissures and hollows carved
by the restless waves.

Farther out, osprey circle above the thrumming ocean,
eyes spying into the deep.

What do they know — the birds?

They stray from meadow to town,
know the freedom of the breeze, the world
a patchwork of greens and blues
that turn into the concrete of ash and umber.

What do they see beyond the soot, the grit —
the neon signs that blink through their sleep?
When morning litters its cups and wrappers,
is leftover bread enough?

Do birds dream of wood carved into cages,
of rain that finds them cradled in nooks of pine and jasmine?

Do they know that rocks sing by the sea,
that crystals spume the air?

That the horizon unfolds the farther they fly?

IF ONLY

Swallows sweep clouds across the blue,
their song a steady advance of summer.
Bloodroot and columbine muscle through layers
of moss, leftover leaves. Honeysuckle
and wild rose lace the air in sweetness.

Knuckled under knots of responsibility,
he clatters his cubicle in the still-gray city.
Walls like rock rise up, close in
as he peeks out a window, catches
a corner of sky, soul trembling with possibility.

When They Grow Up

Sweet gum branches scratch black against paper moon,
swallows sing awake the sun.
Squirrels scrabble the trees, and a crow hesitates
before rising to air, flapping with the breath of God.
Leaves litter the pond, golden patches
on its dark surface serenade winter's return.

Last night my daughter dreamed of white horses —
pounding of hooves that throbbed my room
where I waited for mischievous sleep to tap my shoulder.
Your body warmed mine where I curled
into your back there at the edge of the bed, skin smooth
as polished rock, just as silent.

One last sigh as midnight pushed Evie into her teens,
pulsed my shoulder, and the horses thundered past,
tails panicking the darkness, shattering the dawn.

Return of the Swans

Reeds thorn the river's edge, bleak reflection
of clouds spinning on its surface. Frost
rimes a wheelbarrow's upturned belly, swells
of daffodils rioting through greening leaves.

Sky creases as day gathers night's jagged
lines, erases the stars. Winter's silence severed
by whistling wings and muted bugle calls.

TRESPASS

Silver puddles glint in the half-light, stipple lake's edge.
Hemlocks wade into the water. Branches flirt
with the breeze, crows stenciled on fog. Morning unfurls,

unfastens pinks and yellows from the mountains
one ribbon at a time. Mist dissolves, exposes rotting
fence posts, tumbled trees, three deer. They lift long necks,

noses quivering, before dashing into rhododendron,
dark leaves slapping after them. Soon honeysuckle
will sweeten these woods, sun scald away scented shadows.

But, for now, late winter still speaks in echoing hollows,
in muted dusk.

Storm Watch

Rain sears earth's tapestry.
Spring wind gnashes, birch and oak churn
green fists through yellow-gray skies.

Tornados shift south, shove
between mountain and valley, crisp pine
into blistered needles,
houses and cars rising in brief flight.

Farther north, we track the line
of storms across the screen, wait for your call.
Hear you breathing in the closet.

Ravaged

Yesterday's rain pummeled greening fields,
      fists of irises, tulips now petaled on the ground.

Delta waters tip their banks, level yards
      and neighborhoods with cloudy currents.

Swollen cows drift down streets, boats skim
      attic eaves. Debris girdles posts and cars,

hollows walls, lives.

      But this morning roses still pink the thorns, birches
silver the lightening sky. Chill air flutes with robin-song.

      Mist hovers the lake, mounting sun an echo in orange.

After the Biopsy

Jasmine crawls into the knots, the cracks, surprises
the porch with a leafy screen that steals
heat and light, rises up the eaves, captures rain, despises
my attempts to trim, to cut; it seals
the wind-chimes into silence — curls inside the cups, capsizes
to creep along the rails. Whorls in clusters so thick it peels
the surface, branches twisted to look like lace
until it tears, ripping splinters, gaps — a barren space.

Foundling

We found the baby bird marooned
in oat grass, its brother fractured on the driveway —
long drop from nest to ground.

I caged my hand around its naked
body, eyes still stitched, wings like tiny
toothpicks, useless yet for flight.

Sarah dragged the ladder, tussled it into place
hoping home would heal. I held you — too small
for me to feel your heart beat,

my palm shuddering with your breath.

Fully-Fledged

World hushed inside the car, foothills rise
to my right, black undulations
against gray horizon. A *V* of white lifts,
tugs my attention — geese, sensing the snow-
storm before weathermen.

I called you today — no answer. You are lost
to me. Without your chatter in the car,
on the phone, I feel your absence — the little girl
who loved me without question.

My advice is tempered now, so often
you don't want it. I try to read your moods long distance,
predict your reactions, but I never could.
I once grounded you just to make you
take a stand, rebel. You didn't. Not then.

Now you're far away, ranging higher, farther
than those geese — white specks in an uncertain sky.
For all my doubts, they know where they're going.

Notes Drawn from the River

Live oak and pine stitch the horizon,
shelter the edges of swamp,
Route 10 to Jacksonville a straight line
of scrub, tarmac and bright blue sky.

At the rest stop, cicadas hum
through wild scuppernongs and saw palmettos,
temper water's burble to a minor chord.

Five hours of radio blur my thoughts.
Two hundred miles to go. I reconcile myself
to this quick break to stretch, to blink
away the last few days — a cacophony
of phone calls, packing.

Two blackbirds shadow my lunch,
grouse each other and flap off
when I throw bits of bread. Squirrels taunt
leashed dogs, zigzag grass to rummage
trash cans. I shake out crumbs and walk away
from vibrating asphalt, diesel dissolving,
shimmering in the heat.

Switchgrass leads to loblollies, giving way
to the river. The canopy of leaves and needles
shushes traffic, and a coral snake crawls
over stone, vivid under the Florida sun.

Cicadas, silenced when I broke the tree line,
sing again, forget my intrusion. I stand still
to listen, to relearn the song.

II.

DISCORD

Thunder growls and the dog
whines. Gray clouds
cement the horizon, truncate
afternoon.

A breeze flicks
my face, creases
the long grass, spits dandelion
fluff. Irises wink
at garden's edge, purpling

into shadow. Rain
skeins the sky.

YEAR OF STORMS

Honeysuckle vines slash the air,
jasmine flying. The pier cracks, pops.
Waves rush the shore. Winds punch the coast,
rain and fear spill far inland. Sand and grit spit
at houses that crumble into the flood.

Day dawns a lighter gray, shadows taking form
in drizzling mist. Swallows silenced, feathers droop
in leafy shelter. What the sea releases washes ashore,
coils back into the foam, into the surge,
into the deep.

Propulsion

from *Max Schmitt in a Single Scull* by Thomas Eakins

Sculling the yellow dawn you reach
        and pull, reach and pull. I watch you
from the shore, a tightness in my chest
        as you slide farther away.

Water wrinkles between slip and suck
        of blades — other boaters make way.
Cars and buses grumble behind me,
        sparrows gossip in pin oaks,

roots exposed like nerves, each ebb and flow
        erasing earth. The sky blues and brightens,
unlike yesterday when rain and fog kept
        you home, and I walked along the river alone.

The river bank parts her thighs for you.
        Past the bridge you turn the shell, one oar
resting in its rigger. Muscles in your back stretch,
        constrict — closer, sweat damps your shirt,

your fingers red and rough from the grips.
        Back half-turned to moor, you focus
on the surface, run aground.

Uncoupling

Just after dawn, orange flushes to blue.
Skeins of geese unravel the sky.

Lake muddy after three days' rain,
ducks still drift across its surface.

I drive alone over the bridge, witness
their black and white bodies nip in,

under the water. Why am I always
driving away from you?

You're the one who's leaving.

You're the one who's letting me go.

Right of Succession

Sunlight skims the lake as it sinks behind thinning trees.
On one branch a barred owl, gorget of stripes
beneath a tawny mask, pinions writhing flesh plucked
from scalped fields. Pumpkins burst from seed, green
world transformed orange, amber — harvest's zenith.

Leaves curl, applaud in the brisking breeze. At the dock,
white sails furl, hulls swiveled upside down, keels
lined like dominoes. Soon wet and rot — fusty smells
of winter — will settle in, hazy warmth of early autumn
forgotten, moon rising higher in the sky.

WINTER'S COURSE

I'm missing fireflies this gray November day —
beacons of light, of hope. Stark branches drip

rain. Wind's oboe swells, shudders the last
wrinkled leaves to ground. Swept away

with October's leaves, fireflies no longer
flare twilight. Instead, crows' wings

knife the sky, beaks serrate the black advancing night.

Judas Kisses

the prayer-worn cheek, marks the end
of communion. He's gone too far,
doesn't know how to turn from the path
he's begun. Breath hot, he leans in, inhales
the Sun, Moon, Stars — all creation.

Beneath his thrumming heart, his blood,
he senses a calm not his, a warmth
in the clammy air. Too late. The hammer
of soldier feet, of fate ordained. He drops
his eyes, walks away. Too late.

And in the garden swords, shouts. Silence.

The sun pours a cup of blood-red morning.
Sounds of silver clatter the temple floor.
And on the breeze the rope groans.

Un-Wishing

for Sylvia Plath

The stars fall all around me,
like leaves they brush my face,
and all that's left above
is dark and empty space.

Though Daddy's wrapped with satin,
the worms have made their meal.
Once, twice I tried to join him
and never really healed.

Unfulfilled in London-town —
gray and raw with grit —
when I found you, my god, my love,
my heart discharged its bit.

Our flame flared brief and in the dark
our spirits, too bold, crashed
like mirrors, a clock that cracked,
or blood-red poppies turned to ash.

You led me to a narrow box
with corners tight and small,
gave yourself, then stole away —
I'm like our daughter's doll.

Empty-headed, glassy-eyed,
I try to write but can't.
The night is getting cold, colder,
I choose the final dance.

The stars are falling upward now,
I follow where they lead.
Their silver shards slice hands and heart —
my body ends, my poems seeds.

Landscape in Winter

Tips frosted, evergreens bristle
the mountainside. Ash sky enfolds silent
white. Chilled, I sit at window
and day louvers light through the room.
The clock ticks the minutes, the hours
till I see you.

Frozen roads, ice keep you away. Shadows
shift, fall across the window where I wait,
watching kids across the street build forts,
launch powdery attacks. Their giggles and shouts
whisk the crunching snow, clear air.
Next door Joe tugs his daughter up the hill,
curves behind her on the sled and zigzags down.
Five-year-old wonder bright in cheeks, eyes.

Darkness. The book I assuaged day with drops
to the floor. It's about life and love. Lost.

Amendments

Overnight, a silent winter white
displaced parched, lingering autumn.
Even birds, squirrels haven't emerged
to stir the smoothness of the fields.

Evergreens lean with new burdens, bare
oak and maple cradle nesting snow.
Pulling a blanket around my shoulders,
I turn from the window, watch you sleep.

Too soon this will be gone: plows heaving
up and down the roads, squirrels pilfering
full feeders. I dress, wish you awake.
My footprints a solitary track to the pond.

Unblemished yard slopes to the dusty ice
with its furred crust. Overhanging
trees shelter dark circles around the edges,
black veins fissure its solid surface.

Abandoned

A wheelbarrow rusts
onto snow, metal flakes blush
the white. Gray owl gazes
between pines as snow swirls
the silence. A barn rots,
collapses board by board.

CIRCLING THE EDGE

A dragonfly lingers over the pond, darts
past bog lilies, their pinks blooming
above, through shimmering wings.

Fog veils the far bank, the bridge.
Fracturing the silence, a wood thrush
whistles into dawn.

Somewhere beyond the silvered mist
a pony wrenches tufts of grass.
My eyes return to your face, fingers graze

yours where they clutch the suitcase.
Don't go.

What Whispers Your Name in the Night

It should be snowing by now but isn't —
the north wind exhales its bluster, clouds stalk
stars until no light smolders the darkness.

Gusts chafe the house. As the seconds crumble
toward midnight, toward the new year,
I lie in bed, eyes wide at the ceiling. The past
wrinkles into a heap of guilt and regret.

In cities and parks all over the world, fireworks
rupture the night, champagne tips, people kiss.
Only the wind here, a deliberate choice.

But not mine.

Looking for Ghosts

Dawn's pink fingers unfold lavender
skies — shades of Spring before she arrives.

Another day begins. Are you alone
wherever you're waking up?

Gray fox slips through mist, black tips of fur
a shock of dark in white fog.

Rain blusters into the afternoon, reduces
light to greenish glow. *Days like this*

we went back to bed — cheek and shoulder
caressing — savoring the patter outside.

Rivers rise, gnaw the banks, tentacles
of fear invading the field, the street, the yard.

Dusk drizzles into a wet whisper. Buds crushed,
puddles pour frogs, turtles trench the mud.

Remember getting stuck in the woods — traction lost
in mire and leaves, gaping ruts landing

us in the truck bed watching the sky
grow bright with stars? The river retreats,

vines and trash tangled in streets as lights blink
on, mist smears the darkening night.

Dreamcatching

Breeze shivers curtains, and, above the bed,
the circle sways. Beads, feathers tremble.
I twist under the covers as candles waver
the walls.   Sleep hobbles in.

Web splits. I step into darkness,
feel it encircle me like liquid,
its pressure a pulse against my skin.

Drifting farther, bits of light sputter —
candle flame, stars. I can almost see
your face. A growing hum infuses the silence —
your voice singing — a shadow, an echo
fading as morning breaks.

Settling for Winter

Air splinters with cold, gnaws the moon,
erodes the sky. Snow muffles its hollow
sound. The immortal hour has come and gone,
fir trees rimed, bare oaks crusted white.
Feathers flap the immutable dark,
dive to a scrabble over ice, a squeal, then silence soars.

The North Star smolders as dawn stirs frost.
From across the room, across the ocean, I hear you
breathe, dream of ravens' black shadows overhead.
Their stillness broods over white fields.
Thoughts swirl, refuse to settle in my mind
where the echo of loss blinds like a blizzard.

Scars of Winter

An artist's brush has whisked away gems
of autumn — rubies, topaz fading
to fragile khaki that cracks in the breeze.

                              The last stalks
of goldenrod sway, browning flowers
crumbling into the fields.

Spring, summer, fall have come and gone —
a year since you left. Winter echoes
in the stark and blossomless wood.

                              The forest frowns
into the lake, and flakes write white, light music
on the air.
                    Soon the earth will harden,
drift in robes — an acceptance of snow.

You Will Always Be the Man I Loved

Time, which changes people, does not alter the image
we have retained of them. — Marcel Proust

Every vacation we talked about the beach,
imagined warm swells and gold grit
between toes, lathering lotion on secret parts —
a cool shower together to caress away the day.

One March found us on a foreign shore,
a cold trek with scarves, jackets bunched tight
examining shells without taking hands from pockets.
And then you were gone.

Since then, you and I have walked other shores
with other people, making promises and keeping them.
But the ocean's green-blue glint reminds me
of your eyes. How they shone before you reached

for me. How desire carried us along the years.
How I loved you. And how far apart we are.

TREMORS

Above the tide line I walk the strand,
air pounding my chest in cold gusts.
Remnants of you shadow my steps.

Sweet gums and birches quiver in raw wind.
Winter here, and the sea still sprays
the shore, ice crystals webbing rocks, sand.

You've haunted every breath,
storied my dreams. But now
the throbbing ache withers to a twinge.

Snow retreats in lengthening days.
Sky stretches gray. The season alters
in luminous air and, over the horizon, blue waits.

GOODBYE

Winter staggers into the night,
leftover leaves sputtering a last path
under the Crow Moon — a lonely
tap dance that echoes in the dark.
Fog weaves the valley, ribbons the horizon.

Last summer water lilies swamped
the lake — fat, flat green chained
to muddy bed, dragonflies wrinkling
the water. Under the cedars, sun
and shadow patched your shoulders,
silence pouting into the haze.

Divided by a continent, the seasons flake
away, and spring whispers a new melody,
spiraling through stem and leaf.

Casting Off

She folds paper into angles, tucks edges tight
and sets a votive in the center of this fragile hull.

Honeysuckle brushes her shoulders as she carries her burden
to the pond, stiff folds anchored in her palm.

At water's fringe where butterweed wades with Canada geese,
she crosses the dock and lights the single flame.

Setting the paper vessel adrift, she breathes
it into the current, watches as it burns to ash.

III.

RESURRECTION

Wedges of warmth in April's blue,
cold light scythes the lake.

Ducks cough, waggle into water,
a heron stoops to drink.

Like the hawk, I want to rise —
wings flicking air — burdens

drowning behind me.

EQUINOX

Shadow of sleep still haunts
as clouds and remnants of night
cover the sky. Wind imitates
the river's purl, keeps me in dreams
where I can transform sorrow
                              into laughter.

Light slips into the dawn,
gray ribbons of twilight unraveling
from sight. I wince at your cough
and turn back to the house,
driven by the approaching fall.

Autumn Warning

As summer folds into September,
morning chill curls the leaves. Red tints dogwoods,
gold highlighting oaks, the pines evergreen.
Faded zinnias cradle butterflies, air pulsing
orange, yellow, a bit of blue.

A motor grumbles down the street,
cut grass sweetens the breeze.
A squirrel flashes across the lawn. Another digs
under sweet gums, nut clamped in jaws
as a shadow falls over summer's warm breath.

Wrapped in blankets on the porch, you watch me
sharpen the blade, stack wood. In rhythmic undertone,
a woodpecker hammers the house.
Tropical storms shift south. Crows as large as cats
thrash into the branches, peer into our lives.

Rachmaninoff Suite

Melody in E dimples the air as she wakes,
echoes of an all night vigil stick
to her eyes until she showers — water knocking
a prelude to the morning. Fifteen songs chase
her through the day.

Dust quiets the ivories in the family room.
Once, her husband relished every movement —
would play them each time he caressed the keys —
eyes closed, strings resonating.
Now sun sets through the window.

Facing the building, she breathes
mimosa perfume, sculpted flower beds
pulsing a last chorus of color
before white walls, recycled air claim her.
Urine and ammonia scent the halls.
She ignores whimpers, shouts
as she measures her steps to his room.

Angled against bleached sheets, he waits in silence.
She tugs music from her pocket, turns the dial.
Rachmaninoff charms the room. He doesn't blink.

EVEN THE ROCKS CRY OUT

Good Friday Earthquake, Alaska 1964

Sky reddens, slips into place.
Stillness enters the air. No breath.
Sparrows and chickadees stop chattering.
Kelso's growl wilts to a whimper
as he paces the carpet. Eggs, colors drying,
begin to quiver, dishes picking up
the beat — muted *clickety-clacks* swelling.

The bed shakes me awake,
sleep splintered by shivering walls,
shaking floor. Kelso's barks echo
along the raining roof,
paintings and photographs unhitching.
Baskets shimmy across the countertop,
tumble in pastel kaleidoscopes.

Outside, pines tremble and the river widens,
water rushing the rocks. Starlings take flight
into paling blue. In the woods, leaves whisper,
branches groan and crack.
A fox darts from sheltering trees,
and, across the field, a rooster crows.
Only the dogwoods remain silent.

Unpacking Your Suitcase

Seaweed knots the shoreline, waves
retreating with tide. Clouds bruise the blue
and lightning scratches, a quick fuse.

The gulls are gone, pipers still dodging
froth at water's edge. Wind stiffens
with chill. Salt and sand spit

hard against my skin. The weather
man said *Today, a slight chance of rain.*

BACK FROM HOSPICE

Wind flutes the house
scattering an atlas of leaves.
I watch the gray roll in,
shiver though the heat is on.
I turn out lights.
Listen to the wind.
Upstairs you cough, gasp,
cough again.

Re-Ignition

When you drop into the void,
darkness embraces you
but not oblivion.
Blackness continues to encroach,
to gnaw
at any hope that lifts its head,
its embrace intense.

Scientists say
internal pressure ignites
the birth of stars.
My galaxy should be dazzling,
luminous as noon
with as many stars
as children God promised Abraham.

I'm waiting
for churning clouds
to obliterate memory, thought.
Desire.

I'm waiting for the light.

WAITING

The moon, a thumbnail
scraping sky, vague clouds
torn by black night —
                      I watch you
sleep, shadow stalking light
across your body, blankets
stamped with sweat.
                       Tree sap
hardens and the ants march home,
shrink from frost furring our yard.

CROSSING OVER

for Lisa Stone

Death trembles like butterfly wings, hovers
                               mouth pressed to mouth
My eyes breathe in your body
                embraced in white like on our wedding day
Nurses caress the dog nestled into your side —
Sasha's never been this calm, dark eyes vigilant

A chorus of rain on the window
You smile at me
               Outside, wild roses are beginning to bloom

Prelude

Water pushes its song down the mountain,
crystal shivering on rock ledges.
Ice webs the nearby lake, sharp wind—
silence in blue and white.

Memory ticks a metronome.

Ammonia burns my brain, senses reeling.
White room, white sheets,
your lips tinged blue.
The fermata of machines finally clicked off.

Daffodils, crocuses weave a melody
through the woods,
and the shadow of crows overhead
shrinks under the thawing sun.

SONG OF SORROW

Cup full and flooding, grief kaleidoscopes
into a symphony of pain.
Violins sculpt the melody of loss,
chords kissing the air, my soul.
Cellos linger in a harmony of need,
bass strings throb, my broken
prayer taking shape — scattered notes
forming into one bright, bitter berry,
untasted, unwanted,
trembling until the music fades.

We're Sorry to Have to Tell You

A woman scans the clock, placates her baby —
waves a bear, a rattle, a box of raisins.
His cries inflame the night, startle raccoons
as they grope through ruins of the day.

Flushed with moonlight, the yard's margins
fade, extend to shadows. The gate pivots,
creaks. Footfalls ricochet the path.
Through the window, walls gleam yellow.

The men pause on the stoop, refuse each other's eyes.
Knock.

WITHOUT YOU

The freight train clatters its tracks
at midnight, one, two a.m. The whistles'
restless echo hollows the trees
like surf, like whirlwind.
I watch the clock pulse the minutes,
crawl the hours. Stars score the dark.

What happened to the wood thrush's song,
the crackle of brass leaves
— your heart beat? Daybreak stumbles
beyond the bedroom window, framed
by the perfect silence of this room.

FOLLY

Summer's heat flicks aside the irises,
curls daffodils from gleaming flames
into tanned husks.
Air, moisture-thick, slanders, assaults
my body as I step outdoors.
The sun gloats, ratchets up a notch by noon
and renders its rays across fields, forests,
accepts no falderal from moss and ferns
serried in the shadows.
It was a mistake to think I could outrun
the drying grass, the cracked earth —
memories of you.

Before the Burial

Four mares straddle my sleep —
three dark, one white racing across a frosted field.
Mountains disappear in mist until dawn pinks the horizon,
moon a paper dot glued in blue.

I ache for whispering grass, you to stroke my skin.
As I try to follow, snow cracks beneath my feet,
the white horse stamps, vanishes into ice.

Thunder rattles the house, opens my eyes.
Sullen skies, empty space beside me. Shadows flicker
between flashes. Rain spits the windows, and I rise
in darkness — the long day waiting.

LINES FOR JANE KENYON

A single life weighs less than a feather.
— Japanese Imperial government

Dead a decade, you once ranged these woods
with Gus. Today I wander from New Canada Road
to Eagle Pond where hemlocks hang, no furry friend
nosing the undergrowth. A nuthatch nosedives,
lures my eye to gray and white feathers
forgotten by some itinerant goose. *A sudden stir*
of air moves the sere late summer leaves,
sounding for a moment like . . . rain.

                                      Across Route 4
the white corners of your house wedge half-hidden
behind colossal peonies blushing beside bruised
hydrangeas. A cat spars its shadow in the yard.

As sunlight louvers through trees, I imagine
the wood floors you scrubbed, scarred by generations
of men dusting in from the fields.
Women whose feet ghost through kitchen steam
to skin tomatoes, strip beans, can corn,
whose hands pieced quilts now tucked in trunks.
Quilts packed and layered heavy with feathers,
comforting on icy nights.

Passage

The universe unspins itself, full moon singing
its light across the sky.
Ocean hisses, collapses against midnight,
lingers as the woman struggles through dunes,
wades into water. Mist flecks her face
as she grasps her last treasure, hesitates,
then offers its contents into the darkness.
The tide pushes and pulls.
She lets him drift away in shifting waves.

Slipping back on sand, she settles
against logs that circle the campfire,
tucks the porcelain into a knotty crevice
and watches smoke rise into the night.

When she wakes, a gray dawn shrouds her.
Waves whisk the shore, twist foam and salt
into the air, fringes of seaweed decorating sand.
Fog, white and thick, tricks the light.
Coals smolder orange, an echo of smoky warmth
from night's rhythmic pavane,
from ashes already spiraling the deep.

Hope is a Hard Habit to Break

As twilight shuffles away from chill,
I sip morning and watch a cardinal hop
the edge of the feeder.

Snow and rain thwart light,
mingle gray day, gray horizon.
My lips seek warmth of cup, relish
the burn as it blisters mouth, throat.

Your chair breathes emptiness,
face absent across the table.
The wind shifts.
Cottonwoods bow,
                    forking in new directions.

STRINGING BEES

Sunlight dazzles the lake like a field of bees
sipping its purling surface, wavelets fading
into the water lilies softening the shore.

Again you are not here.
A lacewing butterfly brushes purple loosestrife,
lingers, and I wonder
if you would have held my hand.
A fishing boat drones past,
smoke graying, choking the air
before dissolving to nothingness.

Rhododendron veils the house,
gathers me in shadowy patches of green,
and honeysuckle drifts the breeze.
Light flares, bounces across the water.

Tea cup forgotten on the bench,
I half-close my eyes: glowing specks morph
into golden strings of bees pulsing through time,
                              stitching us together.

Surviving Twilight

I'm past the days of Ouija boards,
Taro cards, begging turbaned
clairvoyants to predict the future,
explain the past.

I will not be a pawn
to memory. I want to lock
myself in the ark, away from storms,
starve these thoughts
until my mind is safe again,
and blank.

The stars are festive, flung
across the deepening night,
dazzling.
Your ghost wanes,
just an airy breath now,

whispering.

IV.

WAKING

Winter puddles, blossom-like.
Gardens of snow skim dreams,
relax the dark, the moonfruit.
Ground thaw giggles
between squirrel and freeze.
Cardinals, bluebirds flower
the gray skies. Listen
as it rises, rises.

Conversion

Not even a ghost could survive here
where echoes of love fracture like ice-
wrapped branches shaking in February's wind.

Gray awning of sky stretches overhead,
fissure of blue breaks through,
sorrow ebbs from the weeping stones,
the wailing desert sands.

Once out of reach, the stars fall heavy,
like sand, rock, sleet.
Melting, wearing away.
Whispers not of ghosts but grace.

Granite, Softened

His rock-hard certainty never eased,
never receded. His look, his distrust
a slab of stone across my spirit.

I never knew his love was so narrow —
a spiny, broken ridge
bound by gullies of suspicion
that left me marooned,
my voice an empty echo
bouncing off his hollow faith.

Funny how a feather thins granite.
How it strokes and smoothes away layers
of secrecy, blame from my stiff captivity.

You fell, settled like a miracle,
like the quiet voice of Our Lady of Lourdes
while I was looking down.

No blazing bush, no blood
or water spilling from a rocky tomb,
no fractured cracks appeared.

Just your touch — a stroke, a caress
until the granite, softened, crumbles —
and, once again, I am light.

THE LANGUAGE OF WATER

after Rachel Rooney

Teach me the language of Water,
currents that run wide and deep,
that glint of gold and wink at noon.
The silver that surprises midnight.
Let my heart embrace rhythms
of forgiveness and forgetfulness.

Teach my mind the way to soften suffering.
When it rises and sprawls
the earth, licks the bark, the vine,
let it tumble back on course, reining
in the might, the muscle of the flood.

Teach me the stillness of reflected dawn,
the faith that wavers when touched
but mirrors truth, kisses the bullfrog
and the dragonfly, ripples into memory.

Don't teach me Stone, the hard core
that sinks into pits, into hollows,
that thins and wears away a sliver at a time.
No, not that. Nothing that can stack and totter.
Teach me the language of Water.

A Fragile Stone

Night puddles, thaws winter slivers.
Garden remembers green
between blue and rain.
Wind whirls autumn browns east
under the swelling sun.
A breath of goldfinches
flicks the feeders as bluebirds—
rusty breasts puffing —
inspect suet. Robins chant from prickling
buds. Sky warms noon, dulls dew
as spring's spell drifts north, assuages
                              the softening fields.

SPRING IS THE HOPE IN ME

Snow still lurks in pine shadows,
edges of the forest trimmed white.
Darkness lingers less each day,
squirrels and raccoons shifting
through stippled light, gray
horizon giving way to icy blue.

The fields, the yards green
in clumps, bones of the earth
massaged by sun. Deep in soil
hearts unfurl, fresh songs leap
from the stream. Moon slides away.

Back in the tree line, a woodpecker knocks.

Return to Happiness

Wind, insistent *shhh, shhh* skidding the trees,
kicks branches blushing with green toward the sky
where clouds tumble across blue. Winter memories sink
beneath a symphony of dogwoods.

Gone the nights when dreams swelled from shadows,
when darkness stretched into loneliness. Tonight
the Crow Moon lifts its wings, sings to the stars.
Lilies of the valley scatter the path, ignite the dawn.

WALKING BAREFOOT

To live is to take off your belt and dance. — Nikos Kazantakis

Catbird mews in the hydrangeas, blue
shadows shielding gray feathers,
clutched grasshopper. Barred owl swivels
its ruff at rustling, wagging branches.

Rain drips onto broad leaves,
spools onto clover tilting purple faces
to the sky. Above shaggy clouds,
a crescent moon sweeps
past Mercury, Venus, Mars
as they dance through the heavens.

Last year my world shriveled to a knot
of pain. Sunlight shunned my rooms,
finches silent in the oaks. But today even rain
holds the promise of…something.

In full passion of the storm I will walk
barefoot through puddles, let the unseen stars
be my guide.

New Love

Moon spotlights curve of road,
trees tucked along its edges.

Frogs baritone lullabies by the creek,
lightning bugs arc overhead.

On the other coast, fires scald and blister.
Across the sea, bullets and bombs flare morning sky.

But, for this moment, I am at peace.
Your hand in mine, we whisper and laugh,

footsteps pulsing with the melody of the night.
A car passes, headlights bright on our faces.

Your hand curves my back. I am not alone.

WHEN I OPEN MY EYES

Something between us
shifted that night.
Now grainy twilight
lessens shadow,
and crows nudge the crocus
in spring's early grass.

Magnolia leaves wax
glossy green, tremble
with morning chill.
Dawn smudges the horizon
and night collapses
as sun and moon rendezvous
in their separate orbits.

A bluebird wounds worms,
and a cardinal, red blazing
with the dawn,
splashes a dew pond.
What astonishes is the singing.

Two weeks of gray finally fracture
into blue. I reach
for your hand. It's already waiting.

Quote by Jack Gilbert

Song Unsilenced

My tongue of silver tarnished when he left.
I watched a moth clap wings, flecks spiraling
to earth. My life suddenly like those specks:
aimless, falling.
The sky a sea,
moon masked under waves of clouds.

Vibrations ripple the air. Somewhere
a flute sings melody, willows sweeping silver clean.
Blackberries tumble at my feet.
I breathe in jasmine, follow
as magnolia blossoms flicker their light.
You wait on the other side.

Recipe for Making the Color Gold

after Nuno Júdice

If you wish to make the color gold,
weigh a handful of coastal sand
and sift it through the noonday sun.
Pour it over the salt-crusted bowl of sea,
stir in flickers of silver fins and floating gossamer domes
until a tart tang zests the air.
Season with scales of the yellow butterfly
skimming above a Jewish ghetto.
To prevent the colors boiling into vapor,
cut the dark heart of a poppy
and toss in two feathers from a mourning dove.
Pluck one peach and two grapefruit
from low hanging branches,
slice ripe corn from green stalks —
peel and grate then blend into the mix.
Fold in the leaf of an autumn oak and four petals
of a daffodil, whisk six violets washed with spring's breeze.
Add a pinch of summer's dry grass to the coin of the moon.
Knead carefully. Measure a large spoonful.
Sprinkle an echo of stars across the night,
and the light of a song will rise with the dawn.

Awakening

Maybe he knows I'm here,
just inside the kitchen window.
The titmouse turns his head, black eye watchful.
He hops into the puddle, baptizes his body
and shakes feathers into fluff.

This morning I woke curled in your arms,
your breath against my cheek in the dusky room,
and I savored your warmth, your desire
for me even in sleep.

When I shifted, got out of bed, you sighed,
mumbled *morning* before twisting the sheet
over your shoulder and turning from me.
What captivates us in half dreams?

It's only eight and already seventy-three degrees,
the Smokies a shadow undulating the horizon.
Overnight, rain rinsed golden dust from the cars,
the porch, and now air sparkles in clear blue.

peter-peter-peter
　　　　peter-peter-peter

Another titmouse flutters to the puddle,
the first darting to the edge. Together
they stir the water, make it ripple and sway —
sunlight leaping from its surface.

ADVICE FROM A HONEY BEE

after Amy Gerstler

Rise from your hive, taste the air
with your wings. Mid-flight find delight
then hum from flower to tree.
Inch to the heart of the matter, drink nectar.
Explore petal and pistil, luxuriate
in gold dust. Share your riches.
Dance. Sting when necessary.
Go home. Shake off the remains
of the day, spin them into thick liquid
that glows when winter comes, warm and sweet.

A Hint of Joy

Here's the joyful face you've been wanting to see. — Rumi

Gulls honk, gannets harp a welcome as day dazzles
the ocean, chases dreams from shadows,
glitter tumbling into the deep.

Last night you sighed my name, called to me
in sleep. Your fingers on my cheek whispered
me awake. Bad dreams again. I feather-touched
your shoulders until your breaths deepened,
warmed my neck. When daylight edged the window,
you were gone — cracked sleep only a puddle
of night clothes on the floor.

I will wait for you to come home,
watch waves measure the shore as day fades,
a string of light on the horizon.
The lyrics of salt air and foam taste of summer —
                              fruit ripening and bursting.

Explorations

Two crows crack bright October's dawn,
finches spinning into the air.
Soon snowflakes will brush the skies,
whisper to the ground with an echo of white.
The chill strokes my skin, lifts
flesh into peaks and valleys.

Across the gorge, maple and sweet gum
flare summer's green mountains into a chain of fire.
Hiking the ridgeline, we see the river curve
below, color shifting as the sun meanders the sky,
first pink then orange, finally brown. A skiff furrows
its surface. Fishermen wade the banks.

I follow you — watch your steps: avoid the rocks
that tremble under your foot, dip under rotting trunks
you slide over, glimpse blazing stars and asters,
goldenrod beckoning along the trail. Pause at leaves
either mountain laurel or rhododendron.
We'll see next spring you tell me, and I smile at your back.

Twilight quickens as we reach the house.
The crows remain, silhouettes in baring branches
as darkness feathers the mountain,
night swallowing their shadows.

What Comes of Waiting

The moth-hour has come,
nutshells fleck the yard
and steam swirls from asphalt
after late rain — a veil
between mountaintop and valley.
Ghost-like wings pearl the darkness,
wind spiraling over barberry and jessamine.

Love and death come on nights like this —
a coolness crackling the air,
sizzle of hope, dread in the owl's sigh.
The spit of rain as it holds back
the moth-flickering moment
before drifting away.

THIS IS WHAT YOU SEE BY STARLIGHT —

shadows nudging stone

    a rake forgotten against the shed, fingers
    etched like rails upon wood

hollyhocks trembling, wind licking
leaf, flower, stem

    distant islands winking, beckoning overhead

doves weeping in hedgerows,
moon lathering the lake

    car creeping in driveway, twin beams blind

clouds stretching, bruising the sky

    a lighted rectangle opening, closing

About the Author

KB Ballentine received her MFA in Poetry from Lesley University, Cambridge, MA. She has participated in writing academies in both America and Britain and holds graduate and undergraduate degrees in English.

She currently teaches high school theatre and creative writing and adjuncts for two local colleges. She has also conducted writing workshops throughout the United States.

Published in numerous literary journals, KB was a finalist for the 2006 Joy Harjo Poetry Award and a 2007 finalist for the Ruth Stone Prize in Poetry. KB also received the Dorothy Sargent Rosenberg Memorial Fund Award in 2006 and 2007.

Learn more about KB Ballentine at www.kbballentine.com.

www.ingramcontent.com/pod-product-compliance
Lightning Source LLC
Chambersburg PA
CBHW032022090426
42741CB00006B/708